flower
pounding

flower
pounding

Linda Rudkin

A & C Black • London

First published in Great Britain 2011
A&C Black Publishers
36 Soho Square
London W1D 3QY
www.acblack.com

ISBN: 978-14081-2746-9

Photography: Linda Rudkin
Design: Susan McIntyre
Cover Design: James Watson
Commissioning Editor: Susan James
Managing Editor: Davida Saunders
Copyeditor: Carol Waters

This book is produced using paper that is made from wood grown in managed, sustainable forests. It is natural, renewable and recyclable. The logging and manufacturing processes conform to the environmental regulations of the country of origin.

Printed and bound in Singapore

Frontispiece: Young leaves of early spring. *Clockwise from top left:* rose (rosaceae), heuchera (palace purple), foamflower (tiarella), spiraea (gold flame), filbert (*corylus maxima*), loosestrife (lysimachia).

contents

acknowledgements

I would like to thank the many people at exhibitions and workshops who asked for this book to be written – and the team at A & C Black, especially my editors Susan James and Davida Saunders, for making it happen.

I am particularly indebted to my friend, textile artist Gina Valentine, for introducing me to the technique of flower trapping, and to Pamela Watts for 'Using Flowers', the first chapter in her book *Embroidered Flowers*.

I would also like to acknowledge the advice and assistance of Dave Johnson, lecturer in I.T. and digital photography.

But I am most grateful, as always, to my husband John for his continued support and encouragement – and for not complaining about the frequent and sustained bouts of hammering in the kitchen, especially while we were on holiday!

Herbaceous border. Geraniums (cranesbill), campanula (birch hybrid) and aubrieta flowers, with various leaves and grasses, hammered on fine, wool worsted fabric. Additional details have been added using a fine-line black pen and hand embroidery.

introduction

'Flower Pounding' hardly seems to be an appropriate title for a book that sets out to show how beautiful images can be produced from flowers and leaves. There is something odd about associating the delicacy and vulnerability of fresh flowers and foliage with 'beating', 'crushing' or 'pummelling', which is how 'pounding' is defined in the dictionary. However, the fact that these lovely images are created entirely by using a hammer, explains why this technique is usually referred to as 'flower pounding'.

I have always depended on the bounty of the garden for my textile artwork, especially since a visit to see the Bayeux Tapestry inspired a love of working with natural dyes. It was in a conversation with a friend about using natural colours that she asked whether I had come across a method of transferring not just the colour but also the shape and pattern of flowers and leaves to fabric by using a hammer! Needless to say I had not, but I was intrigued and after a few lines of enquiry, mostly online, discovered the fascinating craft of flower pounding.

The basic technique is straightforward. It involves placing flowers or leaves directly on to fabric, securing them in position and hammering gently, or 'pounding', so that the colour, shape and pattern bleeds through to the surface of the fabric. This is a very simple way to achieve impressive results and requires no specialist skills or knowledge. Anyone, regardless of age, aptitude or experience, can become a botanical artist in an instant! The only requirement is the ability to use a hammer and a willingness to tolerate a little noise.

Realistically, of course, not every piece of flower pounding will appear as an emerging work of art. For a start, results are not always predictable, but this can be regarded as part of the fascination of this craft. As with all natural colours, results may vary according to the season, the maturity of the plant, and the type of fabric used. Inevitably, some poundings will be disappointing, but 'failures' should not be consigned immediately to the rubbish bin. It is as useful to keep a record of things that did not work well as it is to keep samples of successes. It might be that something that is disappointing to begin with turns out to be usable after all, possibly inviting further work or embellishment. Having cautioned against the expectation that everything will work equally well, it is also the case that you should expect your experience of flower pounding generally to be a source of real delight.

Explaining the simplicity and effectiveness of this technique is as far as most accounts go, but flower pounding has so much more potential to be explored. This is one of my reasons for wanting to write this book. For instance, with a little more thought and careful observation, it is possible to create quite realistic representations of different plants – as well as the more impressionistic images that usually result from first experiments. Pansies and violas, for example, are usually suggested as good subjects for flower pounding because of their strong colours, detailed patterning and flat faces. However, if they are simply placed on fabric and hammered the result is likely to be little more than a rather indeterminate blob of colour. In Chapter Two, you can see how to hammer a pansy so that it looks like a pansy!

Combining the technique with other decorative processes extends the potential of flower pounding even further. Anyone who enjoys stitching their artwork, for example, might add texture and form to their flower pounding using embroidery or quilting. Similarly, the techniques of flower trapping, leaf printing, appliqué and collage, each of which is considered in more detail in Chapter Four, will add interest and another dimension to flower pounding. These are all quite straightforward processes that can be combined very effectively with hammered images to produce unique pieces of textile art.

As a result of my passion for working with natural resources and growing experience of flower pounding, I have been fortunate to work with many groups of people, of all ages and backgrounds. It is usually the case that most members of those groups quickly become flower-pounding enthusiasts and there are a few questions that crop up quite regularly. Specifically, I am always asked whether flower pounding produces washable art and the simple answer is 'no', although hammered images dry-clean beautifully. Flower pounding is also unlikely to be lightfast. If it is important that an image should be washable and resistant to fading then, using a digital camera and a computer, it is quite simple to make an iron-on transfer that can be applied to clothing or linen that is likely to be laundered regularly. There are several other ways of adding permanence to hammered images and these are covered in more detail in Chapter Three. I usually prefer to let nature take its course, knowing that there is always the option of using fabric paint if colour really needs to be restored. However, there is something about the transience of natural colour; the antiqued appearance of faded tones that can have a charm of its own. It is certainly part of the appeal of using flower pounding to make hand-made greetings cards; the gradual ageing of the colours simply adds to the extent to which they are appreciated in an increasingly standardised world.

Another question that is asked quite often is a general one to which I have no satisfactory answer. People ask why, having been enthusiastic craft workers or textile artists for years, they have not come across this technique before. I understand the question perfectly, having been in the same position myself only a few years ago. Perhaps putting this book together is the best I can offer in the way of a response.

Acer hanging (*detail*). Hammered and appliquéd 'leaves' of Japanese maple on silk organza.

1

what you need

1. Equipment

A small hammer A metal hammer with a small head and a long shaft works best and reduces the likelihood of putting any strain on your wrist, arm or shoulder. A good quality, panel pin hammer is ideal and easily obtained from most hardware suppliers.

A wooden chopping board It is necessary to hammer on to a hard surface in order to obtain a clear image. A smooth piece of hard wood, or an old kitchen board, is fine but do check that there are no knots or splits in the wood that might appear as unsightly marks on your images.

Wide masking tape This has two functions: it holds the plant material securely in position while it is hammered and ensures that all the available colour is directed into the fabric. The best masking tape to use for flower pounding is one that is 5cm (2in.) wide and only slightly tacky, so that there will be no trace of adhesive left on the fabric.

Paper kitchen towel This is used to absorb excess moisture from the plant material and to keep the head of the hammer clean. It also guards against making indentations in the chopping board and reduces the level of noise.

Small, sharp, pointed scissors These are essential for trimming plant material cleanly and precisely.

Tweezers It saves a lot of frustration to have these available for arranging tiny or delicate petals and leaves.

Old towelling This is placed under the chopping board to prevent it from slipping. It also absorbs most of the impact and cushions the noise of the hammering.

Left. Equipped for flower pounding in February. Potted ferns, primulas and carrot leaves produce images that combine well at a time when there may be a shortage of usable, fresh material in the garden.

2. Fabric

Any fabric made from natural fibres can be used successfully for flower pounding. It should be white, or at least light, in colour to obtain the clearest results, and washed thoroughly to remove any finishes. It also needs to be well ironed, whilst still damp if necessary, because even the smallest crease can ruin your work.

It is possible to use some synthetic fabrics, and mixed fibres are likely to give satisfactory results, but this is not guaranteed. It is advisable to test small samples first, before committing a larger piece of fabric. It may be obvious, but still worth mentioning, that it is not possible to produce anything other than a patch of damp by using light-coloured plant material on darker fabric.

White cotton sheeting, with a smooth surface, always produces a good outcome. Even small bits and pieces of old sheeting are worth keeping because they are ideal for practising and for testing samples. Old sheets and pillowcases are usually made of good quality cotton with a close weave and have become beautifully white from years of laundering. This makes them perfect for flower pounding and provides an excellent reason to stay in touch with the local charity shop!

Calico and linen take up pigments really well but both have their own natural colour and texture and this needs to be taken into account when deciding which fabric to use.

Silk, or fine cotton lawn, being less absorbent, sometimes allows the colours to bleed beyond the outline, but the softness of these images can be pleasing in itself. These finer fabrics are also useful when working with autumn leaves or any other plant material that contains relatively little moisture.

Fine, smooth, wool worsted usually produces very clear images and deep colours but it has disadvantages: it is quite expensive, not always easy to obtain and often difficult to iron.

Flower pounding dry-cleans beautifully but it is important to note that the impressions are not washable. For 'best' work, and to add as much permanence as possible to the design from the outset, fabric should be prepared by mordanting before use. Although this will still not make the work washable, it will add depth and brightness to the colours and make them more resistant to fading.

If you do try washing your flower pounding, the most likely outcome is that the image will remain clearly visible but the colours will wash out, leaving a biscuit-coloured design. This antiqued effect might be perfect for some projects but, generally speaking, you will want to retain the range of colours, and a number of suggestions for achieving this are covered in Chapter Three.

Fabric samples. *From left to right, top row*: cotton, calico, linen; *bottom row*: wool worsted, silk dupion and silk cotton. Plant material. *From left to right*: pelargonium, aruncus, *lobelia erinus*, soft shield fern (*polystichum setiferum*) and rudbeckia. The brightest, clearest colours are on the cotton; the palest, softest impressions are on the silk.

3. Preparing the fabric

Mordanting is an established part of the process of natural dyeing, but slightly stronger solutions are needed for flower pounding. The mordant acts as a fixative and helps to bond the pigments to the fabric, so that the maximum amount of colour is transferred from the plant material, and the image is made more lightfast.

Alum is the recommended mordant because it will not change the background colour of the fabric, and it is safe to use and dispose of. It is suitable for use with any natural fabric. Alum acetate, specifically for use on cotton, linen and calico, is a little more expensive but worthwhile for the added brightness and strength of colour it produces.

Cream of tartar is used as an 'assistant' with both alum and alum acetate to increase the effectiveness of the mordant and to reduce the amount you need to use. All of these products can be obtained by mail-order from suppliers of dyestuffs. (See the list of suppliers at the end of this book.)

Fabric should first be washed in a detergent and rinsed thoroughly to remove any finishes. It is worth mordanting more than you need for immediate use so that you always have some ready for the next project. However, it is best to work with no more than about 250g (10oz) at any one time because it will be difficult to move the fabric around in the pan and this will prevent it from mordanting evenly.

To mordant approximately 250g (10oz) cotton fabric you will need:

- 50g alum or alum acetate (about 3 level tablespoons)

- 30g cream of tartar (about 2 level tablespoons)

- Water (enough to be able to move the fabric around comfortably in the pan)

METHOD

1. Half fill the largest pan you have available with warm water.

2. Mix the alum with about half a cup of hot water.

3. Stir this into the water in the pan.

4. Mix the cream of tartar with about half a cup of hot water.

5. Add this to the alum water in the pan.

6. Add the wetted fabric as carefully as possible to avoid excessive creasing.

7. Raise the heat slowly to simmering point and maintain this temperature for about 40 minutes, moving the fabric around regularly.

8. Turn off the heat and allow the fabric to cool in the pan.

9. Remove and rinse thoroughly.

10. Drip dry and iron well whilst still slightly damp.

A new mordant bath will be required for each batch of fabric.

The spent alum water can safely be poured onto garden soil as long as it is away from food crops. If poured around the base of hydrangeas, it is said to keep the flowers blue!

4. Plant material

The enjoyment of flower pounding owes nearly as much to the delight of discovering for yourself which plants provide beautiful images as it does to creating usable and decorative pieces of textile art. For that reason, and because it would be an impossible task anyway, there has been no attempt to provide a comprehensive list of suitable plant material to use. However, the following guidelines should help you to experience success from the outset and quickly enable you to anticipate which flowers and leaves will work well, whilst leaving endless opportunity for your own experiments.

FLOWERS

Choose those that have thin petals. Flowers with thick, juicy petals such as tulips, for example, are best avoided because they are likely to squash when hammered, resulting in seepage of colour. Petals, like those of carnations, which are thin at the outer edge but more fleshy towards the centre, need to be reshaped before hammering, by using small, sharp scissors to trim away the fleshy part.

Stronger colours produce the best images, although the colours might change when hammered. Red and pink flowers, for example, often hammer purple. Purple and violet flowers are likely to become more blue, while blue flowers tend to hammer true to their original colour and produce images that are resistant to fading.

Both of these varieties of periwinkle (*vinca minor*) hammered blue.

White flowers have no pigment and therefore will not produce an impression.

Transfers made from yellow flowers tend to be pale and more prone to fading, although there are a few notable exceptions, such as coreopsis, marigolds, rudbeckia and sunflowers, that make beautiful, lasting images. It is no coincidence, of course, that these flowers are also excellent sources of natural dye!

Flowers with patterned petals, like some hardy geraniums and primulas, are particularly rewarding to work with.

Coreopsis flowers.

The strong colours and bold patterns of most primulas make them ideal for flower pounding, especially during the winter when there are few other flowers available.

Hardy geranium flowers produce beautiful impressions when hammered, especially those with prominent markings like this 'Ann Folkard'.

STEMS

Some very fine stems work well but others are either too woody or have too much sap to make a clear impression. It is possible to use a sharp craft knife to slice lengthways down the back of a stem so that the pulpy inside can be scraped away or the sap wicked out, but this is a bit of a fiddly job. You might find a stem from a different plant that can be substituted for one that is too fleshy.

LEAVES

Most leaves will pound successfully. They can be gathered from the garden or hedgerow throughout most of the year. Maples (acers) and ferns, in particular, are wonderful to work with.

Choose leaves that are thin and feel slightly cool to the touch. These are likely to have just the right amount of sap to hammer well.

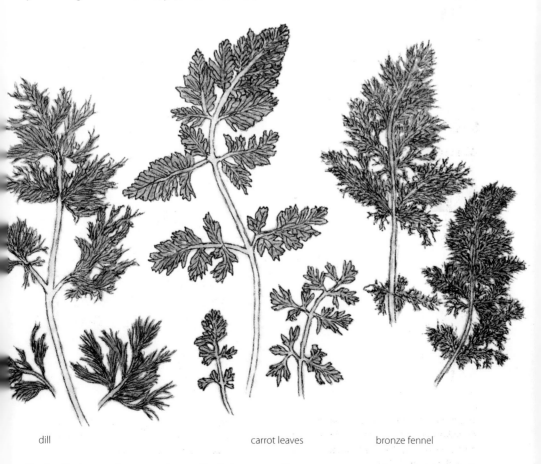

dill carrot leaves bronze fennel

The fernlike leaves of carrots and several herbs hammer well.

A friend gave me some dry maple leaves that she had received from Canada. I rehydrated one between two pieces of damp kitchen towel overnight before hammering it. The resulting impression was clear and detailed but the colour was quite different compared with the original.

It may be tempting to use some fleshy leaves because of their striking colours or patterning, like many varieties of coleus, for example. If you simply place them on fabric and hammer, the colours and patterns will be blurred. Instead, try laying them out singly between two pieces of absorbent kitchen paper and placing them under a book for a couple of hours to remove the excess moisture. If they are left for longer than this they may become too dry to work with, but this method is worth trying for really special leaves.

Conversely, if a leaf that you really want to hammer is too dry to be successful, put it between two dampened pieces of paper towel before placing inside a plastic bag. Leave this under a book overnight. The leaf should rehydrate sufficiently to produce an image.

Leaves that are hard or waxy are best avoided: holly, laurel, and beech leaves are unlikely to yield much colour or produce worthwhile images, no matter how much effort you put in. Mature ivy leaves can also be resistant to pounding but nice, clean impressions can be obtained from the young leaves of early spring.

Look for interesting shapes or patterns. Remember to look at the veining on the underside; it is often quite a revelation!

Opposite: Summer leaves. *From left to right, top: acer palmatum dissectum,* acer 'bloodgood'; *centre: acer palmatum, nandina domestica; bottom:* garden fern, soft shield fern (*polystichum setiferum*).

Heuchera leaves produce good impressions throughout the growing season.

Plants that have variegated leaves throughout most of the year provide excellent material for flower pounding. The impressions tend to be clear with well-defined veining patterns, and the colour and patterning is usually long lasting.

Some plants, such as roses, have a red or pink tinge to their young leaves in early spring as well as in autumn. These are always worth trying because the subtle gradations in colour hammer beautifully.

Autumn leaves are wonderful to work with. They are likely to need more effort with the hammer because they have less sap than earlier in the year, and it sometimes helps to work on finer fabric. The effort is worthwhile because the striking colours are less likely to fade than the green forms of the same leaves.

An extended autumn, particularly one that includes a few warm, sunny days, might encourage some plants to have a second flush of flowers. If this happens after the leaves have started to redden, the combination represents a real bonus.

The variety of autumn colours on this creeping vine (*right*) offers many possibilities for leaf hammering.

Below: The range of colour is reflected in these impressions on wool.

Some grapevine leaves provide stunning images in autumn.

A second flush of flowers on this plumbago (plumbaginaceae) coincided with the changing leaf colours of mid-autumn.

The colours of the leaves and flowers both transferred well.

Do not overlook weeds. There are at least two good reasons why you might decide to allow weeds to grow unhindered somewhere in your garden. First, you might find just the right thing for adding structure or filling a gap in your design; a few blades of grass can be very useful! Secondly, some weeds produce nice images in their own right, particularly those, like feverfew (tanacetum), meadow rue (thalictrum) and herb robert (*geranium robertianum*) that have delicate, feathery leaves, and oxalis, with its clearly defined shamrock shape and deep red colour. Another advantage with plants that insist on growing where they are not required is that, apart from during the depths of winter, they are generally available throughout the year.

Test all plant material on scrap fabric before using in a design. It is useful to write the name of the flower or leaf next to its image and to keep these samplers for reference.

A few grasses added a sense of distance when hammered at the back of this herbaceous border.

2 how to do it

1. The basic technique

1. **Put several folds of towelling underneath the chopping board.** This stops the board from slipping, absorbs vibrations and reduces the level of noise considerably.

2. **Place three or four layers of kitchen towel on top of the chopping board.** This also cushions the sound of the hammering and helps to absorb the impact.

3. **Ensure that the plant material is dry.** If there has been recent rainfall or heavy dew, pat the flowers or leaves between two pieces of kitchen towel to ensure that they are as dry as possible.

4. **Select a flower or leaf.** A small single flower or floret can be hammered whole, but heavier blooms need to be taken apart and the petals re-arranged in a single layer.

5. **Trim away any thick, fleshy parts using small, pointed scissors.** Left untrimmed, these sections will squash and spoil the result.

Trimming away the fleshy base of a mallow petal.

6. **Place flowers or petals face down on the fabric.** Large flower shapes are best positioned and hammered one petal at a time but small, single flowers like vinca, or florets like verbena, can be placed face down on the fabric, trimmed and hammered whole.

Right: Trimming verbena ready for hammering.

7. **Place leaves vein side down.** This usually produces a more interesting and detailed image.

8. **Secure the leaf or petals with wide masking tape.** Large leaves or petals may need more than one piece of tape, in which case it is best not to butt the edges of the tape together because this can cause an unsightly line to appear across the image. Tearing lengthwise down the tape and overlapping the torn edge will avoid this.

9. **Turn the fabric over so that the taped leaf or petal is underneath.** It is often possible to see the plant material through the fabric and very easy at this stage to adjust the positioning if required, simply by peeling away the tape with the flower or leaf attached.

10. **Tap with the hammer.** Tap very gently at first; the image should start to bleed through almost immediately. Increase the force of the hammering only if necessary. Autumn leaves, for example, may need more pounding because they contain less moisture.

Hammering petals of hardy geranium 'Ann Folkard'.

11. Remove the tape as soon as you are happy with the outcome. This prevents any unwanted bleeding of colour around the edge of the image.

12. Continue to add more flowers and leaves until your design is complete.

13. Use a dry iron, at a temperature to suit the fabric, to heat-set the pounded images.

primula

garden fern
(dryopteris)

After removing the masking tape, it can be useful to stick it on to a piece of clear plastic to provide a record of the patterning of the original petal, should you need to refer to it.

nandina domestica

Extra petals are added in stages to produce a clearly defined image.

Finished sampler.

love-in-a-mist
(*nigella damascena*)

oxalis

feverfew (tanacetum)

maidenhair fern
(adiantum)

coreopsis

pelargonium

everlasting wallflower
(erysimum)

fennel (foeniculum)

asparagus plumosus

2. Variations

The flowers that are easiest to work with are those, such as statice or sea lavender, that need no preparation at all but these are only a tiny minority of the flowers that you will want to use.

Also very obliging are any small, brightly coloured flowers with flat faces and thin petals, like primulas, verbena and vinca, that need only the calyx snipped away and to be placed face down on the fabric before taping and hammering. However, the petals of most small flowers fall apart when the supporting calyx is removed and tweezers are likely to be needed in order to reassemble them.

The only preparation needed before hammering this piece of sea lavender (statice or *limonium latifolium*) is to spread the tiny flower clusters out along the stem.

The distinctive flowing form of acers is best represented by hammering groups of leaves on the stem and allowing the overlaps to show. This creates a very natural impression and the overlaps, although visible, are not a distraction.

Right: The flowing forms of *acer palmatum dissectum* and acer 'bloodgood' suggested a natural design for a piece of hammered work.

Below: Overlapping sprays of acer leaves hammered on cotton.

Trim the calyx from the back of *auricula primula* 'gold lace' and the flower is ready to hammer.

Tweezers are indispensable for reassembling the petals of tiny flowers such as aubrieta.

The easiest way to hammer the petals of this spoon-type, spray chrysanthemum bought from a florist, was to tape them down before trimming out the thick, fleshy centre.

Flowers with many petals, such as chrysanthemums, asters and other daisy-types of the family compositae, will just make an unsightly mess if they are hammered as complete specimens. A crisper image can be obtained by taking them apart before hammering and arranging a single layer of the narrow petals into a flower shape. This takes a bit of patience, and a pair of tweezers is really useful, but a single flower will provide many impressions.

Alternatively, reduce the petals to a single layer, place the flower face down on the fabric, and tape the petals leaving the centre of the flower open. Carefully remove the centre using small, sharp scissors and then hammer the petals. When the impression of the petals has dried, a new centre can be added.

Bell-shaped flowers, of the campanula family, produce an indistinct image if hammered double but make charming, delicate impressions when carefully divided.

Divide the bell in half using small, sharp scissors.

The stamens need to be trimmed away but the calyx can be left in place.

Below: Harebells on unbleached linen, outlined with a fine-line pen for added definition.

Harebells (*campanula rotundifolia*) are particularly elegant. I was delighted to find a potted plant, as well as a packet of seeds, for sale at a wild flower nursery because, of course, the flowers should not be picked from the wild.

Daffodils, and other members of the narcissi family, might appear not to be ideal material for flower pounding because the structure is awkward. However, if you are happy to work in profile and divide the trumpet like any other bell-shaped flower, then a very good likeness can be achieved.

The intense blue flowers of *lobelia erinus*, transfer really well and the colour does not fade. Trim away the tubular base of the flower and the small green sepals leaving the three lower petals, with the two tiny upper ones attached. You may need to use tweezers to separate the petals on the fabric but it will be worth the effort as this results in a more interesting shape.

The slightly reflexed forms of these narcissi make a profile that is easy to replicate using a divided trumpet and four overlapping petals.

Lobelia erinus 'Cambridge Blue'.

Pansies and violas make excellent subjects for flower pounding. They have flat, thin petals and come in a range of strong colours with delightful, patterned 'faces'.

However, if a pansy were to be hammered as a complete flower, the colours would bleed into each other resulting in an indistinct blob.

The petals need to be taken apart and repositioned carefully before hammering, in order to produce a well-proportioned and pleasing impression. There are two important things to remember: the first is always to have a complete flower to hand as a guide to construction, and the second is to work from the front to the back.

Starting with the lowest petal, trim away the fleshy base and reshape as necessary.

After hammering the lowest petal, iron it dry. Then position each of the middle petals in turn, using another complete flower as a guide. Pay particular attention to the amount of overlap.

Use the chisel end of the hammer and tap only where you want the image to appear, being particularly careful along the line where the petals meet.

Sweet peas (*lathyrus odoratus*) produce cleaner, more delicate impressions three or four days after picking, which means that they can be placed in a vase and enjoyed for their beauty and fragrance until they start to wilt. Absorbent fabric works best; beautiful impressions can be obtained on cotton but the results are blurred on silk. The most realistic effect is achieved by working in profile. The petals must be divided in half and hammered separately. The calyx can also be cut in two, and a small craft knife used to slice off a thin sliver of stem. Each bloom will produce two images, which, when placed on opposite sides of the stem, create quite a life-like impression.

Pansies on cotton.

Half of the upper petal of the sweet pea flower is hammered first. The lower petal segment is placed in an overlapping position but hammered only where the impression is required.

Sweet peas (*lathyrus odoratus*) hammered on cotton.

3. Useful tips – and a few other suggestions

- **Do not aim for too much realism in your flower designs.** Most work better after being dismantled and reassembled on the fabric before hammering – and this may result in a 'new variety'.

- **Sometimes the leaves of a flower that pounds well are too large or fleshy to be used successfully – so mix and match.** For example, ferns and maple (acer) leaves always hammer well and make good foliage for many flower shapes.

- **Flower centres can be problematic** because they are often very thick. If you want to make a centre, try cutting a small piece from a leaf or petal of a different colour, or trim off the tops of dark-coloured stamens and sprinkle these in the centre of your flower before taping and hammering as usual.

- **If you want petals to overlap, allow each one to dry before hammering the next.** This often results in lovely designs because the outlines and shapes of both petals remain visible. This is also a good way to add interest to a design when working with paler coloured petals.

- **During the hammering process, wipe the flat surface of the hammer frequently so that unwanted colour is not transferred to the fabric.** Brushing the hammer lightly on the kitchen towel at regular intervals is all that is needed to keep your fabric clean, but it is especially important when working with deep-coloured petals.

The lower petals of these salvia flowers were trimmed and rearranged to make something completely different.

The subtle differences in colour of these single, spray chrysanthemum petals, were even more effective when overlapped.

- Sometimes, leaves and petals transfer **solid matter to the image as well as colour.** This should be allowed to dry so that it can be scraped away with the blunt edge of a knife, or thumbnail, without smudging. Alternatively, press the sticky side of a piece of masking tape on to the image; the dry debris should lift away cleanly on the tape.

- **The strongest colours and clearest patterns are usually revealed when the masking tape is removed.** For this reason, it is always a good idea to apply the plant material and masking tape to the same side of the fabric; a small piece of tape in a corner of the fabric will serve to remind you which side this is! However, there is no right or wrong side to your pounded work; there is simply whichever side you find most pleasing or suitable for your project.

A soft, dry paintbrush comes in handy when trimming the dark stamens of a sunflower (helianthus) to make a new centre.

3 next steps

1. Making a composition

Put leaves in position 'behind' flowers.

Hammer the leaf only where you want it to show. Use the chisel end of the hammer along the edges where the leaf joins the petal.

Up to this point, we have looked at ways of creating hammered images of single flowers and leaves. When planning a design involving a combination of two or more items, some thought needs to be given to the order in which the separate elements are hammered. If the complete design were to be assembled before doing any hammering, the overlapping areas would appear as double images. This would result, at best, in elements of confusion within the composition and, at worst, areas of blurred outlines and muddied colours. The solution is to work in stages, beginning with the foreground and working backwards. This runs counter to our painterly instincts but it enables all elements to be hammered so that, for example, leaves appear to be behind flowers, without creating a double image at the point of overlap.

This process is suitable for any composition, simple or complex, that includes overlapping elements.

1. **Decide which components are going to be in the foreground** of the design, and behind which all other items should appear.

Vinca minor (periwinkle) flowers and leaves.

2. **Put these in position**, remembering always to place the plant material and masking tape on the same side of the fabric.

3. **Tape and hammer the foreground elements.** Allow these to dry – or use an iron, set at a moderate temperature to avoid scorching the image.

4. **Position the next layer of plant material**, i.e. the items that you want to appear to be immediately behind the foreground, and tape in position.

5. **Hammer only where you want an image to appear.**

6. **Add any further layers**, working progressively towards the back of the design until it is complete.

Summer jasmine leaves (*jasminum officinale*). The stem on the left was hammered first, followed by the one on the right and then the stem in the centre.

2. Enhancing and embellishing images

Flower pounding can be enhanced or embellished by adding definition, detail, colour or texture using pen, paint or stitch in any combination.

Outlining with a fine-line pen is perhaps the simplest way of adding definition, shading or additional detail to your work. It is also a useful way of rectifying outlines where a petal or leaf colour has bled beyond where it was expected. Suitable pens are available in a range of colours, but a black 0.5mm liquid ink pen is probably the most useful.

Any colouring medium can be used to enhance hammered images, depending on whether or not the work needs to be washable. If it needs to be washed, then proprietary fabric paints or acrylic paints, heat set by ironing, should make the image washable by hand. For work that will not be washed, choose any colouring medium that suits your purpose.

Hammered designs can be quilted very effectively. The stylised shapes and simplified outlines of petals and leaves lend themselves readily to hand-quilting techniques.

Embroidery, by hand or machine, offers almost unlimited scope for adding colour and texture to flower-pounded textiles. It is a particularly effective way of creating a centre for a flower because the stitching provides a focal point and adds textural interest.

Applying paint to an image is often easier after the fabric has been stitched. The lines of stitching form a barrier that acts as a check to the movement of the paintbrush and helps to prevent the paint from travelling beyond the boundary of the design. This is particularly the case when an image has been quilted; the raised contours of the fabric make it much easier to keep the paint within the outlined shapes.

Alpine strawberry leaves produce lovely impressions, especially in the early autumn when the colours begin to change, but can benefit from some added definition.

Pelargonium flowers and two varieties of acer leaves hammered on cotton. Extra definition and texture has been added using a fine-line pen, stitching and beading.

Detail, left. The beaded and stitched flower centres are the focal point of the arrangement.

Rose leaves are inclined to lose their colour fairly soon after hammering. These were quilted along the veining lines before being painted.

3. Making images permanent

The colours of a hammered image are neither lightfast nor washfast. Exposure to the light for any length of time will cause most colours to fade to paler, more muted tones. More interestingly perhaps, if you wash a hammered image, the design will remain crisp and clear but any variation in colour will be lost and the entire image will become biscuit-coloured. Even at this stage, of course, it is possible to restore the colour permanently using fabric paint, with the design still clearly visible. This is as easy as painting by numbers!

Flower poundings will dry clean beautifully, losing none of their colour at all. In fact, the process is likely to heat-set an image. However, it will still be susceptible to fading if exposed to strong light for any length of time or if it comes into contact with water.

The safest way to make a permanent image of an original flower pounding is to use a digital camera and a computer. There are many products available for transferring images on to fabric. These offer the opportunity not only to incorporate hammered designs into washable items, but also to apply them

Sweet peas (*lathyrus odoratus*) printed on silk habotai treated with *Bubble Jet*. The original flower pounding (see p.40) was given more definition using fine-point liquid-ink pens. It was photographed with a digital camera and, using an editing programme on the computer, the contrast was increased to compensate for the softening effect of printing on silk.

to different coloured backgrounds. Some, like 'Image Maker', involve making a colour photocopy and then painting this with a solution before placing it face down on the fabric and soaking away the backing paper. This works well for smaller designs, but it is difficult to achieve a consistently good quality of transfer over a larger area.

Easier and quicker to use are the iron-on ink jet transfers which are printed directly from the computer by selecting the 'iron-on transfer' option and 'photo' quality in the printer settings. The images are then ironed onto the fabric using the hottest setting on the iron. Packs of these transfer sheets are readily available from stationers and supermarkets, but an important point to bear in mind when using any of these is the significant loss of texture and fabric softness that usually results because the transfer sits on top of the fabric giving a smooth and slightly glossy finish, which may or may not suit your purpose.

Bubble Jet, on the other hand, is applied directly to the fabric. It comes in liquid form and is said to be suitable only for 100% cotton or silk, but also works successfully on fine, smooth wool. The fabric needs to be saturated in the solution for about five minutes: a large, inexpensive roasting tin is perfect for soaking an A4-sized piece of fabric and avoids using more *Bubble Jet* solution than necessary. The fabric is then allowed to dry before being ironed on to the smooth side of a piece of freezer paper and trimmed to fit into an ink jet printer. Supported by the paper, the fabric feeds through the printer without difficulty, making it possible to print digital images from the computer directly on to the fabric. After printing, the ink needs to be allowed to cure for at least 30 minutes and preferably 24 hours. The freezer paper can then be removed and the image fixed by washing and rinsing the fabric, using either a mild detergent in cold water or a solution of *Synthrapol* which will help to fix the inks and ensure the removal of any surplus colour that has not completely penetrated the fibres. This method takes a little more time and effort, and is only suitable for small projects but, because you are printing directly on to the fabric, the softness and texture of the fibres is retained. It is possible to buy pre-treated fabrics ready for printing, but they can add considerably to the cost of a project with little or no difference in the quality of the print.

Plumbago (plumbaginaceae) printed on cotton treated with *Bubble Jet*. As with the sweet peas (*left*), a clearer print was obtained by increasing the contrast of the digital image before printing.

# combining flower pounding with other techniques

1. Leaf printing

Printing with leaves produces an image of the veining pattern that is less substantial than a hammered image from the same plant. When positioned to give the impression of being behind the arrangement, the printed leaves will appear to be more distant.

MAKING LEAF PRINTS

The pliability of fresh leaves makes them ideal for printing. A leaf may not feel very robust when picked, but the more times it is coated with paint, the stronger it will become. The most interesting prints are produced from the underside of a leaf, especially if it has a distinctive veining pattern.

WHAT YOU NEED

- **Suitable leaves**. It helps to leave a short length of stem attached.

- **Acrylic paint**. This has a good consistency for printmaking and works well. Watercolour paint or dye can be used but it needs to be mixed with gum arabic or a similar substance to make it thick enough for printing.

- **Soft-bristled paintbrush**. One with a flattened end will help to spread the paint thinly and evenly.

- **Plastic sheet**. The transparent panels cut from the front of gift boxes are excellent for printmaking, but any smooth plastic surface is fine.

- **Paper or fabric**.

- **Kitchen towel**.

Hammered, printed and quilted primula flowers and leaves.

Fresh leaves with a clearly defined veining system make particularly effective prints.

Coating a leaf with paint.

Applying the print.

Revealing the leaf print.

HOW TO DO IT

1. Spread the undiluted paint thinly and evenly on to a smooth, water-resistant surface such as a plastic sheet cut from packaging.

2. Place a leaf, vein side down, on to the paint and press lightly all over with a fingertip.

3. Lift the leaf carefully by the stalk or rib and place on the surface to be printed.

4. Cover with a folded piece of kitchen towel and keeping the stalk end secure in one hand, smooth firmly and evenly all over with the fingertips of the other.

5. Remove the kitchen towel and lift the leaf away cleanly and carefully by the stalk.

The same leaf can be reused to produce many prints because it will be strengthened by successive applications of paint.

It is also worth experimenting with making a second print from the same leaf without adding more paint. This requires you to work quickly before the paint dries, but the ghosted image that it produces can be used very effectively to add further depth and interest to a design.

ADDING PRINTED IMAGES TO FLOWER POUNDING

One of my workshop participants commented that she thought printing was quite a high-risk strategy for a piece of hammered artwork – and she was right. However, it can add another dimension to a simple motif and is quick and easy to do.

HOW TO DO IT

1. Test the leaf on scrap fabric to check that it will produce a good print.

2. Decide exactly where the printed image is to fit and trace the outline of the hammered design at that point.

3. Place the tracing over the front of the leaf and cut carefully along the traced line to produce a piece of leaf of exactly the right shape to fit.

4. Print in the usual way, using tweezers to avoid unwanted smudges as the leaf is lifted away from the design.

Printing looks most effective against a hammered image if the same types of leaf are used.

Testing a filbert (*corylus maxima*) leaf.

A section of leaf cut to fit the hammered image.

Printed leaves add more depth to a design.

Hammering *acer* leaves on silk organza.

Opposite. Acer hanging. Hammered and appliquéd acer leaves on silk organza – with brazilwood-dyed silk dupion and wool worsted behind.

2. Appliqué

The idea of combining appliquéd shapes with flower pounding offers a solution when blemishes in a piece of work need to be disguised; necessity, as usual, being the mother of invention.

Having discovered that it is possible to use quite fine fabrics successfully for flower pounding, I decided to make a wall hanging of silk organza using the hammered leaves of two varieties of Japanese maple (*acer palmatum dissectum* and acer 'bloodgood'). Each leaf needed only a very light touch with the hammer to bring the image through but, unfortunately, this was still enough to distort the weave of the silk in a few places.

The only way of rescuing the work was to use appliqué. Using a few of the leaves as templates, the shapes were cut from scraps of dyed silk, backed with *Bondaweb*. Once these were ironed into position on the hanging, the distortions in the weave were concealed and, by way of an unforeseen bonus, the stronger colours of the appliquéd leaves added depth and perspective to the design.

Overleaf. Hammered and appliquéd daffodils (narcissi). The yellow flowers of spring tend to fade quite quickly and so the colours were made more permanent with dry watercolour pencils before the motifs were cut out and machine stitched to the background fabric.

3. Flower trapping

This lovely technique was explained to me by textile artist Gina Valentine, who demonstrated the process of flower trapping and recommended the right resources to ensure a successful outcome. Thanks are also due to Pamela Watts, who describes the technique of trapping petals in the first chapter of her book *Embroidered Flowers*.

The technique uses fresh plant material and, like flower pounding, works best with flowers and leaves that are not too thick or fleshy. It can be combined effectively with hammered images by using these to create a background for the trappings. With a little care and a fine, sharp needle, trapped flowers and leaves can even be stitched!

WHAT YOU NEED

- **Baking parchment**. This will protect the iron and the surface of the ironing board.
- **Backing fabric**. Any fabric with a smooth surface is suitable, including synthetic.
- **Fusible webbing (*Fuse FX*)**. This is available by mail order and is recommended for the fineness of its gossamer-like fibres which disappear from the face of the work when it is ironed. Other makes of fusible webbing, such as *Bondaweb* and the slightly finer *Mistyfuse*, work equally well, but they are likely to remain visible as a light frosting on the surface of the finished work.
- **Fine chiffon**. Fine, white, synthetic chiffon scarves are better for flower trapping as they are much more transparent than silk chiffon. They are readily available, inexpensive and quite economical to use.
- **Small, sharp scissors**. These are used to trim away the fleshy sections of petals and leaves.
- **Tweezers**. Use these to position petals and leaves when accuracy is required.
- **Iron**. Use a craft iron or an ordinary domestic iron without steam.
- **Plant material**. Choose thin, dry petals or complete flowers. Similarly, any leaves that are not too fleshy should work well. Flowers with some patterning give very pleasing results e.g. primulas, pansies, violas, alstroemeria and nasturtiums. Hydrangea florets trap beautifully.

HOW TO DO IT

1. Start making a sandwich with a piece of baking parchment as the bottom layer.

2. Place a piece of backing fabric or paper, right side up, on to the baking parchment.

3. On top of this place a single layer of fusible webbing.

Streptocarpus flowers trapped on handmade paper.

Equipped for flower trapping. Thin, colourful petals and delicate leaf shapes are ideal for this technique.

4. Arrange the plant material carefully face-up on top of the webbing. If you are making an arrangement, try to prevent items overlapping, because when the work is finished, darker material will obliterate anything lighter placed over the top, and stems will almost certainly remain visible behind flowers and leaves.

5. Cover the plant material with a second piece of fusible webbing.

6. Lay a piece of fine chiffon over the top.

7. A second piece of baking parchment completes the sandwich.

8. With the iron set for 'cotton', iron the sandwich several times, front and back, until it is completely flat.

9. Remove the top piece of parchment. If the webbing is still visible, try increasing the heat of the iron slightly, taking care not to scorch the plant material by holding the iron in position for too long. Do not forget to replace the baking parchment first!

Trapped flowers and leaves can be applied easily to a printed or darker background. Using baking parchment to protect surfaces, iron a piece of *Bondaweb* to the backing fabric before cutting out the trapped motif. Remove the backing paper and iron on to the new background.

Alstroemeria petals, trimmed and rearranged with maidenhair fern leaves (*adiantum fragrans*) on top of fabric and fusible webbing.

The trapped arrangement of alstroemeria and maidenhair fern leaves (*adiantum fragrans*).

The overlapping petals of a coneflower (*rudbeckia fulgida*) were trapped and applied to a printed cotton background. The flower centre shows machine- and hand-embroidery.

ADDING TRAPPED MATERIAL TO FLOWER POUNDING

There are at least two ways to do this. The hammered work can be used as the background for the trapped material or you might choose to produce the two pieces separately and then combine them; this safeguards against the risk of spoiling your hammered work by making a mistake with the trapping. To do this:

1. Plan your work, at least in your head if not on paper.

2. Complete the hammering.

3. Make the trapped arrangement separately so that it will fit where required on the hammered background.

4. Iron a piece of *Bondaweb* on to the back of the trapped work.

5. Leaving the backing paper in position, cut out the trapped design.

Blue hydrangea florets, trapped and stitched, with hammered, painted and quilted hydrangea leaves on woad-dyed wool.

6. Iron the trapped work into the required position on the hammered background.

This method was used to put together a panel of blue hydrangeas worked on wool. The very fine wool worsted had been dipped briefly into a woad bath to echo the blue of the flowers. The hydrangea leaves were hammered in a square, leaving the centre open for the flowers. Woad paint was added to some of the leaves where the colour had not transferred well. The florets were arranged and trapped into a shape to fit the design, cut out and applied to the background using *Bondaweb*. The centres and edges of the flowers were edged with buttonhole stitch before the veining patterns of the leaves were quilted. The quilting pulled in the fabric and pushed the central flower panel up like a cushion; just another of those 'happy accidents' that people who work experimentally with textiles are occasionally blessed by!

USEFUL TIPS – AND A FEW OTHER SUGGESTIONS

- Be prepared to take liberties with the structure of a plant when you reassemble it as part of your design. All flowers will appear to be completely flat and this means giving some thought to which parts to use and how to place them in relation to each other.

- Quilting around the edges of petals adds another dimension to a design.

- If you are assembling a large or complex arrangement for trapping, work on your ironing surface from the outset to avoid dislodging items when the work has to be moved.

- Consider using petals in their own right, to pattern or even cover a surface. In her book *Embroidered Flowers*, Pamela Watts describes how to make a delightful gift bag using rose petals bonded onto silk.

Hammered images, or trapped flowers and leaves, make lovely greetings cards, but you may get mixed results hammering directly on to card because the image tends to fragment. This problem can be overcome by ironing the hammered image on to *Bondaweb*. It is then very easy to cut it out, remove the backing paper and iron into position onto a blank card. Alternatively you could simply use a card with an aperture and enclose the hammered fabric behind it. Making cards from trapped flowers and leaves is even simpler – just use a blank card in place of the backing fabric.

Greetings cards. *From left to right:* hammered verbena flowers and leaves; hammered maidenhair fern (*adiantum fragrans*) with trapped verbena flowers; hammered aruncus leaves with trapped hydrangea florets.

4. Collage

Of the countless textile artists who are inspired by the world of nature, many will find that they are unable to resist collecting bits and pieces of interesting debris such as seashells, skeletal leaves, broken fossils or shards of bark. With the luxury of a bit of storage space, the collection can become a valuable resource for creative work. This is the justification for concluding this book with some examples of 'collage', defined in the dictionary as 'any work put together from assembled fragments', because it provides a rationale for incorporating these precious remnants into new projects.

Hunstanton beach from the cliff path. The photograph has been printed onto cotton treated with *Bubble Jet*. The herb robert plant (*geranium robertianum*) was hammered and colour added for more impact before being ironed into position behind the broken fence using *Bondaweb*. Bits of dead, twiggy plants and seed-heads were used to echo the late summer grasses on the cliff-top and to unify the design.

The peeling bark of an ageing eucalyptus is added to my collection when small pieces fall to the ground.

Ivy (*hedera helix*) on eucalyptus bark (*eucalyptus gunnii*). A photograph of the eucalyptus bark was printed onto cotton fabric that had been treated with *Bubble Jet* before adding texture and shading with machine stitching. The fresh ivy leaves were trapped between cotton and chiffon, backed with *Bondaweb* and ironed into position. The addition of a small fragment of eucalyptus bark completed the collage.

Sea lavender (*statice latifolium*) and honesty (lunaria). Sprays of sea lavender were hammered on to natural-dyed cotton sheeting and stitched. Then honesty seed-pods were trapped between two pieces of chiffon to preserve their structure and translucency before being applied with a tiny amount of fabric adhesive. Finally, a few sprigs were tied with raffia and glued into position.

5 gallery

Pink hydrangea panel. The pink florets in the centre of this panel have been trapped and appliquéd to the hammered surround. A few flowers were trapped separately and allowed to 'fall out' of the centre on to the brazilwood-dyed, habotai silk background.

This piece was worked in the autumn and the imperfections that develop as the flowers age creates additional effect and interest. Single French knots stitched in pale silk thread represent the tiny centres of the hydrangea florets.

Hydrangeas lose their colour quite quickly after being hammered but the shapes and outlines in this example remained clear for a sufficiently long time to apply definition with a fine-line pen. The design was then quilted and used to provide a contrasting background for the pink florets arranged in the centre on the panel.

The depth of colour and markings on the petals of geranium 'Ann Folkard' transfer beautifully when hammered.

The inclusion of some imperfect material adds realism to a design. The flower centres have been embroidered with French knots.

Geraniums 'Ann Folkard' hammered on unbleached linen. The colour of geranium leaves is short-lived, unlike the flowers, which retain their depth of colour for a very long time. Watercolour pencils, used dry for greater subtlety, have been used to redress the balance.

Alstroemeria petals arranged over hammered asparagus fern (*asparagus plumosus*).

This design involved using a piece of hammered work as background fabric.

Asparagus fern leaves were hammered on to cotton that had first been mordanted with alum acetate. The next stage was to cover this fabric entirely with a layer of *Fuse FX* webbing before trimming and arranging the alstroemeria petals.

After adding another layer of webbing and a piece of chiffon, the flowers were ironed into position.

Some of the alstroemeria leaves were cut in half lengthways and trapped separately before being sewn into position. The stalks were painted using a watercolour pencil, and stitched. To finish the flowers, the petals were quilted and the centres stitched with French knots. The fern leaves were also stitched for additional colour and texture.

Opposite: The finished piece, embroidered and quilted.

This piece (*above*) was worked simply for the pleasure of using the flowers of perennial flax (*linum anglicum*). Throughout the summer months, these intense blue flowers last for a single day, falling to the ground by late afternoon. The plants are becoming increasingly rare in the wild in England and, of course, should not be picked. I bought my plant from a local wild flower farm and it settled very happily in a pot.

The flowers were hammered on fine wool worsted that had first been mordanted with alum. The grasses were then put into position and hammered 'behind' them. The work was completed using both hand- and machine-embroidery.

Left: Only the flower centres were hand-stitched; machine-embroidery was used everywhere else.

Opposite: Flax flowers (*linum anglicum*) and meadow grasses (*detail*).

Poinsettia cushion; *detail right.*

The stylised shapes and simplified outlines of petals and leaves lend themselves readily to hand quilting techniques. These large 'flowers' are actually the red bracts of a fading poinsettia that was rescued on its way to the compost bin after Christmas. The five smaller bracts were hammered first, followed by the larger ones around the outside. Silk habotai was used to produce softer, more muted colours.

After ironing *Bondaweb* to the back of each flower, it was quite easy to cut away the centre line of each petal and attach a piece of white silk to the back to form a stripe. This was emphasised with a line of running stitches. Both flower shapes were then quilted using thin wadding and cotton backing fabric. The outlines were couched with hand-dyed silk bouclé threads and the centres embroidered. Then the flowers were appliquéd on to a brazilwood-dyed silk cushion cover. Finally a discharge paste was used to remove some of the dye from the cushion cover and 'echo' the shapes of the petals.

Above: Original image with computer-printed transparency. *Opposite*: Cyanotype of hammered image with added stitching and beading.

Ruth Brown's excellent book *Cyanotypes on Fabric* provides all the information needed to learn how to produce a photographic blueprint on fabric. Put very simply, the process involves working in subdued light and painting your choice of natural fabric with a mixed solution of two chemicals (available in powder form by mail order). When the fabric is dry and has been ironed, a 'resist' is applied to create the design. This can be in the form of small objects, plant material or, in this case, a computer-generated transparency of the hammered, red design of pelargoniums and acers from Chapter Three, converted to 'grayscale', with heightened contrast, in a photo-editing programme.

This image was created on treated cotton. The transparency was positioned on the fabric and secured in a clip frame. It was then exposed to the bright sunshine of a midsummer day for about ten minutes. At the end of that time, the frame was taken into a room with subdued lighting (the kitchen worktop behind drawn blinds) and the transparency removed from the fabric. Then the fabric was rinsed thoroughly in clean water to wash away the chemical solution and reveal the detail of the design. Over the next 24 hours, the exposed area deepened further to this lovely Prussian blue. After ironing, the fabric was backed with thin wadding. The outlines and mid-ribs of the leaves and edges of the flowers were hand-quilted, and the flower centres stitched and beaded, to provide a focal point for the design.

conclusion

When I started to write this book, I was not certain that there would be enough to say about such a simple technique. However, it has been an ongoing process of discovery. As I compiled each section, I found new possibilities or ways of improving techniques. Each time I lead a workshop, the participants bring not only different plants, but also their own ideas and approaches for using them. This results in a refreshingly different 'show and tell' of designs at the end of each day – a valued source of inspiration for which I am very grateful.

The process of flower pounding continues to inspire and delight me – and the immediacy of the results is the reward. Finding a new plant that hammers well continues to bring the same sense of satisfaction that accompanied my earliest experiments. I hope that this book will encourage you to share my enthusiasm for what can be achieved so simply and easily – with little more than a few flowers, leaves and a hammer.

glossary

Acrylic paint Water-based, fast drying paint suitable for use on textiles. Acrylic paint can be heat-set by ironing.

Alum (potassium aluminium sulphate) General purpose mordant, suitable for all types of natural fabric and applied before colour to improve take-up and fastness.

Alum acetate Mordant specifically for use with cellulose fibres such as cotton and linen.

Appliqué The application of any other material to a background fabric.

Baking parchment Non-stick baking paper.

Calico Hardwearing and inexpensive cotton cloth usually speckled with tiny seeds.

Calyx Whorl or ring of leaves forming the outer case of a bud or the envelope of a flower.

Collage Artwork in which three-dimensional items are attached to the surface, usually by adhesive.

Cream of tartar Used to make a mordant more effective and thereby reduce the amount needed.

Cyanotype A photographic image created by sunlight on treated fabric to which a resist has been applied.

Discharge paste Used to remove dye from natural fabrics.

Embroidery The use of stitch to embellish a surface.

Freezer paper Used to support fabric for computer printing.

Fusible webbing Gossamer-like, iron-on adhesive, used to bond fabric surfaces together.

Gum arabic (gum acacia) Binding agent or thickener, used with watercolour paints, inks or dyes.

Lawn Very fine, lightweight cotton fabric.

Leaf printing Adding the veining pattern of a leaf to a design by applying paint to the underside of the leaf and impressing on to the surface of the fabric.

Linen Cloth woven from flax. It has a distinctive oatmeal colour in its unbleached state.

Masking tape Easily removable tape that is only slightly tacky.

Mordant Metallic salt used in natural dyeing to attract and bind pigment to fabric.

Quilting Stitching simultaneously through three layers: the surface fabric carrying the design, a layer of thin wadding and a backing fabric.

Sepal One of the divisions or leaves of the calyx of a flower.

Silk dupion Medium-weight silk fabric with a firm texture and slub in the weave.

Silk habotai Lighter-weight, very soft silk fabric generally used for silk painting.

Silk organza Sheer, almost transparent, fairly stiff silk fabric.

Synthrapol A mild, low-temperature detergent used to remove excess dye, printer ink or finishes from fabric.

Worsted Fine, smooth, non-hairy woollen fabric that takes up colour beautifully.

bibliography

Brown, Ruth, *Cyanotypes on Fabric: A blueprint of how to produce…blueprints!* (Sunk Island: S. C. Publications, 2006).

Frishkorn, Ann, & Sandrin, Amy, *Flower Pounding – Quilt Projects for all ages* (Concord, CA: C. & T. Publishing, 2000).

Martin, Laura C., *The Art and Craft of Pounding Flowers* (Emmaus, P A: Rodale Inc., 2003).

Watts, Pamela, *Embroidered Flowers* (London: B. T. Batsford Ltd., 1995).

list of suppliers

Anglian Furnishing Fabrics
(natural fabrics)
40 Magdalen Street,
Norwich, NR3 1JE
Tel. 01603 624910
Web. www.anglianfashionfabrics.co.uk

Ario
(chiffon scarves, transfer mediums,
printable fabrics, fusible webbing)
5 Pengry Road,
Loughor,
Swansea, SA4 6PH
Tel. 01792 529092 or 01792 429849
Email: fiona@ario.co.uk
Web: www.ario.co.uk

ARTVANGO
(Fuse FX, chiffon scarves, fabrics,
transfer mediums printable fabrics,
Synthrapol, *freezer paper)*
1 Stevenage Road,
Knebworth,
Hertfordshire, SG3 6AN
Tel.01438 814946
Email: art@artvango.co.uk
Web: www.artvango.co.uk

Doughty's
(cotton sheeting fabrics, including
'pre-washed', cotton lawn, silk)

3 Capuchin Yard,
Off Church Street,
Hereford, HR1 2LR
Tel. 01432 265561
Email: sales@doughtysonline.co.uk
Web: www.doughtysonline.co.uk

Naturescape
(wild flower plants and seeds)
Lapwing Meadows,
Coach Gap Lane,
Langar,
Nottinghamshire, NG13 9HP
Tel. 01949 860592
Email: sales@naturescape.co.uk
Web: www.naturescape.co.uk

Oliver Twists
(natural fabrics)
22 Phoenix Road,
Crowther, Washington,
Tyne and Wear, NE38 0AD
Tel. 0914 166016
Email: olivertwistsretail@fsmail.net

Rainbow Silks
(fabric, paints, transfer mediums, Synthrapol*)*
85 High Street,
Great Missenden,
Buckinghamshire, HP16 0AL
Tel. 01494 862111

Email: caroline@rainbowsilks.co.uk
Web: www.rainbowsilks.co.uk

Stone Creek Silk
(book and kits for making cyanotypes)
Stone Creek House,
Sunk Island, Nr. Hull,
East Yorkshire, HU12 0AP
Tel. 01964 630630
Email: ruth@stonecreeksilk.co.uk
Web: www.stonecreeksilk.co.uk

The Silk Route
(silk fabrics)
Cross Cottage, Cross Lane,
Frimley Green, Surrey, GU16 6LN
Tel. 01252 835781
Email: hilary@thesilkroute.co.uk
Web: www.thesilkroute.co.uk

George Weil & Sons Ltd
*(mordants, fabrics, paints, transfer
mediums, freezer paper, Synthrapol,
fusible webbing, cyanotype kits)*

Old Portsmouth Road,
Peasmarsh, Guildford,
Surrey, GU3 1LZ
Tel. 01483 565800
Email: esales@georgeweil.com
Web: www.georgeweil.com

Whaley's (Bradford) Ltd
(fabrics, including wool worsted)
Harris Court, Great Horton,
Bradford,
West Yorkshire, BD7 4EQ
Tel. 01274 576718
Email: whaleys@btinternet.com
Web: www.whaleys-bradford.ltd.uk

Winifred Cottage
(chiffon scarves, fusible webbing)
17 Elms Road,
Fleet,
Hampshire, GU51 3EG
Tel. 01252 617667
Email: sales@winifredcottage.co.uk
Web: www.winifredcottage.co.uk

index

More Textiles Handbooks

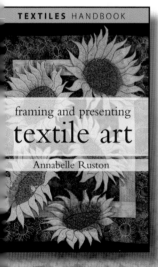

TEXTILES HANDBOOK

mixed media &
found materials

Lucy Renshaw

9781408101032 • £15.99

www.acblack.com/visualarts

A&C